The Art Of Stock Picking

For Common And Uncommon People

The new legendary handbook for learning how to invest and win in the multi-trillion dollar stock market.

Terren Richard Faloh

The Art Of Stock Picking For Common And Uncommon People

Copyright Page

By Terren R. Faloh (c) 2019 United States of American

Reproduction or translation of any part of this work beyond that permitted by Section 107 or 108 of 1976 United States Copyright Act without the permission of the copyright owner is unlawful. Requests for permission or further information should be addressed to the author, Terren R. Faloh TerrenRF@tutanota.com.

This publication is designed to provide accurate and useful information in regard to the subject matter covered. It is sold with the understanding that the publisher is not engaged in rendering lega, accounting, investing, or other professional services. If legal advice or other expert assistance is required, the services of a competent professional should be sought.

M.S.R.P. $19.99

Nothing in this text is to be construed as investment advice tailored to any specific person, statements or characters in anyway similar to real people are purely coincidental, no character featured in the text is necessarily a real person but probably is.

If you don't like this book, may God have mercy on your soul.

Dedication

To everyone who has contributed to my education and didn't get any credit throughout this book.

Preview Page..

"The information is available in this book:

"How to get rich and crazy explanations by the author… all in the author's opinion"

If you think that sounds crazy, let me explain the next part to you..."

On Page 10

"A share of stock is how society keeps track of the ownership of a public company?

Yes, you are quite precocious, as it turns out. Public companies you may have heard of include Apple, Inc, Microsoft..."

On Page 14

"How do I tell if I am picking stocks the right way?

Easy. Whether or not your picks went up over a three-to-five year period of picking stocks to buy. That's the criteria for a stock picker. Now you know how to check your progress along the way.. Easy!"

On Page 16

The Art Of Stock Picking For Common And Uncommon People

**"Stock Picking 101
Surveying The World Of Finance**

Earlier, I mentioned Warren Buffett got rich in the stock market through a cycle of buying low and selling higher. That's the trick to turn in order to get richer.."

On Page 20

The Art Of Stock Picking For Common And Uncommon People

Table Of Contents

Welcome Letter 1, Second Welcome Letter

Section 1: Groundwork

The world of investing and financial markets.

Stock Picking 101: A Discussion Between Newbie McSlick And The Stock Market Genie

Surveying The World Of Finance

Surveying The History Of Finance

Sir Isaac Newton Was Unsuccessful In The Stock Market

Examples Of What A Successful Stock Pick Looks Like

Examples Of Pitfalls To Avoid In Stock Picking

Section 2: Knowledge

What To Do, And, Especially, What Not To Do

Digression On Stock Picking And A Ward Against Bad Advice

How To Win In The Stock Market

The Arts And Technique Of Stock Picking: Money In Minus Money Out

Appendix: Playing Ball With Peter Lynch's Advice From 1988

Detailed Table of Contents

"The information is available in this book:...4
"How to get rich and crazy explanations by the author… all in the author's opinion"...4
        Welcome Letter 1, Second Welcome Letter...6
    Section 1: Groundwork...6
        The world of investing and financial markets......................................6
        Stock Picking 101: A Discussion Between Newbie McSlick And The Stock Market Genie..6
        Surveying The World Of Finance...6
        Surveying The History Of Finance...6
        Sir Isaac Newton Was Unsuccessful In The Stock Market....................6
        Examples Of What A Successful Stock Pick Looks Like......................6
        Examples Of Pitfalls To Avoid In Stock Picking...................................6
    Section 2: Knowledge..6
        What To Do, And, Especially, What Not To Do....................................6
        Digression On Stock Picking And A Ward Against Bad Advice...........7
        How To Win In The Stock Market..7
        The Arts And Technique Of Stock Picking: Money In Minus Money Out..7
        Appendix: Playing Ball With Peter Lynch's Advice From 1988...........7
Get the answers to:...11
People Who Have Made It In Stocks..11
The information is available in this book:..15
"How to get rich and crazy explanations by the author… all in the author's opinion"...15
How A Stock Price May Go Higher Or Lower Than It Is Today..................26
Sir Isaac Newton Was Unsuccessful In The Stock Market!........................33
A Digression On Stock Picking And Ward Against The Assault Of Non-Investing Ignoramuses..36
    Money In – Money Out = Business Earnings.....................................36
        Business Earnings ÷ by # Of Shares Company Stock Outstanding = Earnings Per Share..36
Protecting Your Portfolio From Yourself..37
Here's how to do it. Win in the stock market..38
Company Management Is Not Your Stock Picker......................................39
An Example Of Management Deception By Omission Of Information.......40

The Art Of Stock Picking For Common And Uncommon People

The Price Of A Stock You Own Will Do Whatever It Wants..........................42
No Margin Loans..42
0. • Money In – Money Out = Business Earnings..50
That is the formula: Money In – Money Out = Business Earnings...............52
Cash From Operations – Cash From Investing – Tricked Up Cash From Financing = Business Earnings..52
Hot Tips for Stock Picking From Various Opportunities..............................53
I Figure I Will Tell You About Myself To Potentially Help You Gain Perspective...56
Non-Symmetries In Life...56
    Understand the nature of the companies you own and the specific reasons for holding the stock ("It is really going up!" doesn't count.) 61
    By putting your stocks into categories you'll have a better idea of what to expect from them..61
    Big companies have small moves, small companies have big moves..61
    Consider the size of a company if you expect to profit from a specific product...61
    Look for small companies that are already profitable and have proven that their concept can be replicated..62
    Be suspicious of companies with growth rates of 50 to 100 percent a year...62
    Avoid hot stocks in hot industries...62
    Distrust diversifications, which usually turn out to be diworseifications...62
    Long shots almost never pay off..62
    Its better to miss the first move in a stock and wait to see if a company's plans are working out..63
    People get incredibly valuable fundamental information from their jobs that may not reach the professionals for months or even years...........63
    Separate all stock tips from the tipper, even if the tipper is very smart, very rich, and his or her last tip went up..64
    Some stock tips, especially from an expert in the field, may turn out to be quite valuable. However, people in the paper industry normally give out tips on drug stocks, and people in the health care field never run out of tips on the coming takeovers in the paper industry....................64
    Invest in simple companies that appear dull, mundane, out of favor, and haven't caught the fancy of Wall Street...65

Moderately fast growers (20-25 percent) in nongrowth industries are ideal investments..65
Look for companies with niches..65
When purchasing depressed stocks in troubled companies, seek out the ones with the superior financial positions and avoid the ones with loads of bank debt...66

Welcome Letter

We'll begin with the big idea here – to get you richer. Maybe you are not even rich yet, but you can get a leg up by saving money and having your money working for you. The art and the craft of intelligently picking stocks to buy is simple enough anyone who passed elementary math can do it.

The cardinal rule for making money in stocks is the same as in any business: Buy low, sell high!

This manual is the playbook for getting a good deal on your stock investments.

Everything you need to know about stocks from the bottom-up is covered in this book!

Get the answers to:

What is the stock market?
Why does the stock market exist?
How do people like me make money in the stock market?
Where does the money go when I lose in stocks?
How do I know I am getting the right, *low*, price for a stock?
When do I sell the stocks I buy?
And so much more..

People Who Have Made It In Stocks

The Art Of Stock Picking For Common And Uncommon People

Thousands of everyday people have lifted themselves out of the rat race and gathered great wealth for their families through the art of buying low and selling high in the stock market.

Famous names in this area include Warren Buffett and his partner Charlie Munger, who have made substantially all of their enormous wealth from scratch through the art of buying low and selling high in stocks. Did you know the famous Oracle of Omaha ran a series of investment pools (popularly known as Hedge Funds) and made other people rich along the way? Well its true – that's how Warren Buffett made it into the real big leagues of the uber rich. If he had stayed on his own, investing his own savings into his stock picks over the years, he'd only have become a millionaire one hundred times over. Maybe that doesn't entice you..?

Sometimes I have to think a lot about how I am going to present this material to you, the audience, because from my perspective on this stock picking thing.. picking winning stocks is like *shooting fish in a barrel*! And I want to make it that easy for you, too. So I decided to call this book <u>The Elephantine Book Of Stock Picking</u>.

And hey.. when there is an elephant in the room, who's talking about it? All the partygoers are worried everyone else already knows about the elephant and will call you an idiot for mentioning it. But I tell you what, if you're trekking through the jungle of life.. You can do a lot worse than riding on the back of an elephant!

So, I invite you to continue with this manual and learn the art of buying low and selling high in stocks.

The Art Of Stock Picking For Common And Uncommon People

Second Welcome Letter

My writing style is called imperial, and always comes off at least somewhat patronizing.

If you have read J. K. Rowling's Harry Potter series, I put this style in the category of "Probably How Tom Riddle's Diary Was Expressed To Molly The Ghost". Only, of course, I am not the fictional character Tom Riddle. I have always rather admired Harry Potter's courage, and that of his friends as well, over the antagonists of the series.

The point is – I am not writing in the modern Novel format. This is not a 3rd person narrative, most of the time, I am writing to you from the Point Of View Of This Book. That's it, these conclusions are not portable to any other purpose. The book is just itself, this book, intended to deliver information in a format reasonably and safely digestable by the normal human brain.

So you see, I am embodied with the book and this text seeks to conquer (relatively) empty spaces where the reader has room to learn something. And this is the approach I have selected in order to deliver the best distilled form of information I have made available to you through this book.

Basically I am saying: Don't take anything I have to say seriously. I write conspiracy theory information here in these pages because I think conspiracy theory is fun. I include all of the information in this manual for the purpose of making this opportunity known to you:

The information is available in this book:

"How to get rich and crazy explanations by the author… all in the author's opinion"

If you think that sounds crazy, let me explain the next part to you:

I think you might be imaginative and imagine this book is in a space (3rd eye imagination) and this book is there in the imagined 3-D Space, and the jacket of the book is Green. You won't be able to return to this point often because of my amazing writing style that will keep you glued to read on clear through the next page, nonetheless, you will enjoy life more if you at least mildly exercise your imaginative powers and actually endeavor to deliberately use your so-called 3rd eye's imaginative powers in order to make a space in your mind where you are free to do something so simple as imagine the image of a green-jacketed book as I have described above.

Everything I have ever read has stuck with me. And that is super impressive, on account of my having read thousands of words over the years.

Returning to the imagined green-clad book, I have to mention this book spits fire. Everything in this book may be wrong, based on deceit and mystery. Most likely everything in this book is out dated. So let me spoil the conclusion: A business is valuable based on how much money it brings in over its necessary expenses.

When the above conclusion is invalidated, this whole book will turn into a garden snake. That's right, the imagined book will become a green garden snake.

This book is written in order to make it clear where the chance to spot businesses for sale is. If you buy a business and it produces $1,000,000 (that's one million dollars) for you, that might be good for your bottom line. Otherwise, your name is Warren E. Buffett (more on him later) and another $1,000,000 added to the bottom line is too small a figure for you to be concerned with.

A toast to your success in stock picking.

-Terren

Section 1
GROUNDWORK
The world of investing and financial markets.

A Discussion Between Newbie McSlick

And

The Stock Market Genie

This first part of the book I am going to treat you like a total newbie. I won't hold your hand too much throughout this text, but those of you picking up this book and learning about the stock market for the first time are going to need these introductory lessons.

We are going to start with some question and answer. Throughout the ensuing dialogue, many of your answers will be made plain to see. Our questions will come from Newbie McSlick and the answers are from The Stock Market Genie.

As you can see beginning on the next line, we start with the basics of the stock market, the conversation moves on to investing and we wrap this introduction to the stock market with some comments from Newbie McSlick and The Stock Picking Genie.

What is a "stock" in the "stock market"?

The Art Of Stock Picking For Common And Uncommon People

We all know shares of stock are traded in the place called the stock market.

Stock is what a company is made of, if you were going to hold the company in your hands. In an established company, you have the supplies for doing business: you have a stock book of business & business relationships, you have a stock of trade secrets, a stock of real estate, possibly a factory, or equipment assets, and, of course, you have the stock of money in the company.

Everything I just listed is part of a company. A stock is a share in a company. When you own stock in a business, you own a share of all the stuff the business owns. One share of stock is usually about .001% of a business, because of the small division of the shares, many people may own some shares of stock in the same business.

The nice thing about stock in a company is every one of you people who own the company gets treated equally. Your .001% of the business is going to go up or down in value just as much as the guy who owns 1% or 25% of that same business. Of course, whatever liabilities the company has also have to be taken into the reckoning. More on reckoning the business earnings is in Section 2: Knowledge.

Basically, stock investing is the act of buying, holding, and possibly selling, shares of a business trading on the public market.. In order to get more money than you had before.. from the stock picker's point of view we are looking to buy low and sell high just like anyone else.

A share of stock is how society keeps track of the ownership of a public company?

Yes, you are quite precocious, as it turns out. Public companies you may have heard of include Apple, Inc, Microsoft, Dow Chemical, 3M (the makers of branded high quality duct tape, among other things), McDonalds, Best Buy, and many more.

Who can own a share of stock in a public company?

Anyone, basically. Anyone who opens up a brokerage account and pays the money to buy any of the stocks trading on the market.

Who is Warren E. Buffett?

I am so glad you asked.

Warren E. Buffett (W.E.B.) is an American businessman and investor. You have probably heard his name because he became one of the richest men in American during the late 20th Century and has remained one of the richest men clear through 2019, the year this passage is being written. While I have not met the man, I will refer to him as Warren throughout this brief history.

Warren was born in Omaha, Nebraska to a middle class family. His business career is a story arc right out of the American Dream playbook: A person steadily working from the bottom of the totem pole on-up. He began delivering news papers as his first job in his early teenage years and was lucky enough to be imbued with the idea to save his money.

So he kept accumulating the pennies he earned for each newspaper thrown onto the driveways of the neighborhoods he peddled through on his paper boy route, and, having saved his money plus grown tired of tossing newspapers he began his career as a businessman.

By the time he was 18 he was already an experienced Bubble Gum Machine Operator. He used those newspaper pennies to buy Bubble Gum Machines, then rented locations in stores and made his first profits in the local confections game.

However, bubble gum machines are not what catapulted Warren to fortune and fame.

Ultimately, his vehicle to fortune was the stock market where he bought shares of businesses that were selling for a low price and could generate enough profits or dollar value to create a return on investment. Then, his process for stock market investing goes, he'd hold onto the stock for higher prices until the opportunity came along to… Sell the stock for a 20% or more gain on his original investment! Wow! Warren is smart, but he didn't invent the idea of, "Buy low and sell high".

Warren's stock picking skills took him from small town Omaha entrepreneur to one of the richest men on the planet.

What is a bid and ask? What is a stock market auction?

Trading shares of stock takes place through an auction process where buyers make offers for shares of stock and sellers post the price they're willing to sell the stock. The buyer's offer is the "bid" price, and is below or at the market price for the stock, the seller posts their price called the "ask".

Supply and demand?

Since a stock company's trading price is the result of the latest transaction between a buyer and seller, the amount of buyers versus sellers is "matched up" through the auction process and if the market gets hot and buyers are competing with each other for more of the same trading stock, its only natural the sellers will ask for a higher price per share of stock. This also works in reverse. No buyers, lower stock prices.

In summary, the buyers supply the demand and the sellers supply the stock.

The SP500, the NASDAQ, and the DOW? I have heard them called Stock Market Indexes. What are these things?

Stock Market Indexes are bunches of different stock companies piled together based on their valuation. Buying a stock market index is like buying into a haystack because there is definitely a needle or two in the haystack.

Stock picking is knowing how to use an X-Ray machine to get the needle you want out of that haystack. I pass on the indexes.

How do I tell if I am picking stocks the right way?

Easy. Whether or not your picks went up over a three-to-five year period of picking stocks to buy. That's the criteria for a stock picker. Now you know how to check your progress along the way.. Easy does it along the way, it takes time for the stock market to bring up a beaten down stock.

Stock Picking 101

How The Stockpicker's Opportunity Arises

In this chapter we will delve into the reasons for how come the opportunity to make money in stocks exists.

Earlier, I mentioned Warren Buffett got rich in the stock market through a cycle of buying low and selling higher. That's the trick to turn, over and over again, in order to get richer through shares in public companies.

The opportunity for a stock picker to find a low price is partly because the future *is* uncertain, so there will be times when fear and panic have driven away all of the stock buyers and only the well informed and brave will buy the shares, and partly the opportunity to buy stock for a low price appears because the financial markets are more than just the stock market.

Sometimes things outside of a specific company will bring down the stock market as a whole and a few good stock picks by a well informed investor are likely to pay off big time during such episodes.

Let's state the stock picker's opportunity again: There are times when certain companies are trading lower than the value of expected future cash flows the business seems on track to generate. The stock picker buys in at the low price, holds, and sells at a higher price. That's it!

The key here is to buy 100 shares of stock for $25 and sell them for $30 or $40 per share and pocket a gain of 30%+ or more. If your stock pick is a real home run, the kind you feel in your gut and have done your homework on, buy the 100 shares of stock at $25 and hold until you can finally sell 10 shares for $150 a piece in five-to-ten years from now and hang onto your other 90 shares worth $13,500. A fortune relative to the original $2,500 investment.

Big home runs don't come along often, but there are a number of people who bought Apple, Inc stock back when Steve Jobs walked the Earth. A great stock pick and everything working out so well like it has for many Apple, Inc investors doesn't come along everyday. Its still worthwhile to keep in mind that over the long Apple, Inc story, many Apple investors made over 100 times return on their pick.

How A Stock Price May Go Higher Or Lower Than It Is Today

How is it possible that a stock price is lower and then higher or vice-versa? Is that even conceivable? Well, here are a few reasons stock prices change up and down over time. The amazing common sense of these scenarios will shock you, no doubt. Use your imagination:

• Business picked up because McDonald's ran a super advertising campaign, so the company is selling more burger. fries, & soda, making more money than ever before. Investors bid up the price of the stock. Voila, higher stock price following the improvement in earnings at Mickey D's.

• A new search engine from an unknown start-up replaces Google and takes their ad business. Profits at Google go down, investors sell their stock and have to ask for less and less because there are no buyers for the shrinking business this season.

• Wells Fargo gets caught doing something shady and slapped on the wrist with a monetary fine. The company's profits continue to grow but bad press leads thousands of investors to sell and buyers aren't forthcoming, because most intelligent investors loathe investing in back stock, so the stock price goes down.. in the short term.

Each of these may be a stock picking opportunity as they happen, or during the aftermath where you'll typically have some time to sort out the reality of the situation and do your stock picking 'homework'.

Stock Picking 101

Surveying The World Of Finance

Earlier, I mentioned Warren Buffett got rich in the stock market through a cycle of buying low and selling higher. That's the trick to turn in order to get richer with stocks. The opportunity for a stock picker to find a low price is partly because the future *is* uncertain and partly because the financial markets are more than just the stock market.

Before we cover the other big businesses in the field of finance, let's state the opportunity again: The stockpicker's chance to get rich is when a stock's price is trading lower than the value of expected future cash flows the business is expected to generate and the stock picker buys in at the lower price, holds, and sells at a higher price. That's it.

Well, this stock market thing is a big business tied into the heart of the financial industry. The other big playing fields include Bonds, Currency, Futures, and Options. I provide a summary of these businesses in the table below:

Big Businesses In The Field of Finance	What Its About
Stock	Ownership of businesses: Valuable operations and assets.
Bonds	Collecting interest on loans secured against assets.
Currency	Trading the money to buy stuff in different geographic locations and nations. The oldest financial market.
Futures	Securing the ability to sell an asset at a certain price sometime in the future.
Options	Contracts to buy and sell a stock at a certain price from today through 'til contract's expiration date.

Since this book is about stock picking, we are going to concern ourselves with how the other major fields of finance might effect our #1 concern as pro stock pickers and trainees. That #1 concern being: How are the operating earnings of businesses we invest into coming along?

One thing I can't emphasize enough is that Stocks are Shares in a Business. Therefore, the stock market is a selection of over 9000 different businesses offering the public the chance to buy a piece of their operating business or the businesses and assets in their possession (such as real estate or an inventory stocked with gold bars, paper towels, oil rigs, etcetera).

Here's how each major field of finance might contribute to our stock picking experience:

Financial Field	Relevance to Stockpicking
Stock Trading	General fear and loathing may lower demand, enthusiasm and hype may increase demand. Troubles in the world that don't affect our company's operating profits may cause the shares price to go lower or higher for periods of time.
Bonds	Interest expenses or other burdens associated with carrying debts may cause bankruptcy for our stock company, leading the price to $0.00
Currency	A business might earn 50% of its profits in American Dollars and 50% of its profits in Euros, and lose half

of its business value as the U.S. Dollar strengthens overtime (or vice-versa). A business may earn 100% of its sales revenue in U.S. Dollars and may effectively cancel most currency risks.

Futures & Options These will effect the stock's price, sometimes we see a certain stock go very high or very low in price partly due to the influence of these markets, though, they won't harm our stock picks in the long run.

Stock Picking 101

Surveying The History Of Finance

Each of the financial markets I mention in the table, the Stocks, Bonds, currencies, Futures, and Options, have a long and storied history. There are so many amazing things and fascinating events taking place throughout the history of these markets.

Remember, everything that has ever happened in modern civilization has taken place in parallel with the existence of the stock and bond markets, being that the Western World has had stock markets for over 600 years, tracing its history backwards through time from New York, to London, to Paris and so forth.

Currency trading is the oldest of the major fields of finance, tracing a history that existed long before Jesus of Nazareth walked the Earth and money changers were operating in the Temples.

Therefore the long history of money and finance is rich with intriguing events not only in its own right, what with the well-known big market meltdowns and the global financial crises of the 2000's.. Seemingly unrelated parts of history get drawn into picture. For what steady mind is able to tease out the difference between the collapse of the rather wicked East Indies Trading Company's trading stock issue of the 1600's and Sir Isaac Newton's decision to publish the Principia Physica?

Sir Isaac Newton Was Unsuccessful In The Stock Market!

All I know about that part of history is the tidbit that Isaac Newton put most of his life savings into the Dutch West India Company Stock right before it crashed and wiped out most of his estate! That was a huge bubble priced stock way back in Newton's day, before the steam engine was invented.

Maybe the stock market took away the "easy money" from Sir Newton, in order that he may focus on his true purpose in the fields of physical sciences? Yet another history of cause-and-effect which will remain a mystery for all time.

And what if the world did not get Sir Newton's book when it did.. Well, who knows? Maybe we'd still be plodding around without the mighty steam, combustion, rocket thruster & jet engines, let alone the electric light bulb, washing machines, computers, space exploration, and so on.

I think you get the point about the rich stories in the history of the stock market, and how the market has played a role during momentous occasions that your school textbooks just didn't mention.

This briefing on Sir Isaac Newton, a verified genius with an astounding production, also goes to show you there is risk in the business of investing into stocks.

Good thing you are reading this book and therefore being prepared to become a great, or even greater, stock picker – which you may become, whether you are or are not destined to become a legendary genius like the star of our story, founder of classical physical mechanical sciences and the co-inventor of calculus, Sir Isaac Newton.

Section 2

KNOWLEDGE

What to do and, especially, what not to do.

A Digression On Stock Picking And Ward Against The Assault Of Non-Investing Ignoramuses

The way to pick stocks successfully is to do so independently. you're reading this book in order to learn how to do just that. Onto stock picking facts.

The way to pick stocks is to know what you are doing as a stock buyer, and what you're doing as a stock buyer is investing into businesses. And business is basically simple:

Money In – Money Out = Business Earnings

The value of a share of stock is based on the Business Earnings, in the long-term:

Business Earnings ÷ by # Of Shares Company Stock Outstanding = Earnings Per Share

The secret sauce is to never forget what you're doing in the stock market. This isn't for entertainment, its for getting rich. Oddly enough, that means doing nothing with your stock holdings for long periods of time. Like months, and often enough when you've got a winning stock, long periods of time means holding for three, five, ten, or forty years, when you have a company that continues to prosper.

Re-read this book or go on a dinner date and catch a movie if you want entertainment.

Protecting Your Portfolio From Yourself

Don't add your stock tickers to your phone, and don't use a broker. A broker is no one's friend, he is an enemy stationed in the belly of the beast (the Financial Industry). His job is to call you up and convince you to trade exclusively for the purpose of generating the commission revenue necessary for his next trip to Maui. Avoid all stock picking advice like the plague because those stock market commentators probably didn't read this book or any other quality book on the topic of getting rich investing into businesses.

Don't indulge the advertising-driven stock promoters doing visual arts voodoo such as the so-called technical analysis of charts the actors on MSNBC present. Hollywood and youtube et al. have more valuable things for you to watch than the non-local news channels, these days.

Don't lend your ear to the bad advice these stock chartists give.

Don't give an inch to an anti-investor, they'll take a mile.

If your brain is mush up 'til now, let the contents of this book be the one hard thing you've got. This book is the perfect stock picking microchip, so don't let your time learning the contents of this text be wasted by the corrupting ideas about the stock market told to you by some ninny who wants to slow you down and turn you away from that part of your destiny as a successful stock picker and investor.

As the famous activist investor Carl Icahn once said,

"If you want a friend on Wall Street, get a dog."

Here's how to do it. Win in the stock market.

Keep your eyes open for companies that are under the radar of most Wall Streeters.

You don't need more than ten companies in your portfolio.

Buy companies that will be able to pay back your investment over time, even if the stock doesn't get any attention from Wall street. The stock price is not the company. The Money In – Money Out formula is the company, for our stock picking purposes.

Don't sell growth stocks too soon. Doubling your money is not a good reason to sell when you may be on track to get a four, ten, or twenty times return. Don't hold on to companies that already started out big when realistically they won't be able to grow enough to double or triple their earnings, so if you're in a big company sell at a gain of 30 or 40%.

Company Management Is Not Your Stock Picker

Don't give management's speeches any credit, the CEO is an actor nine-times-out-of-ten, graduated from the rebranded community colleges called the Ivy League. Management's allegiance is to themselves and their allies are the Board of Directors, oftentimes the equivalent of a Corporate Deep State. That is just one way to see it as an outsider looking in, browsing for a place to put our money to work. All of the aforementioned title holders (Management, including the CEO, and Directors) collect pay checks redeemed for cash from the company, just for showing up.

Ignore the so-called "Pro-Forma" and "Adjusted Earnings" or other figures found outside of the audited financial statements. These "Adjusted" numbers are tools management uses to hide losses resulting from bad decisions they made or straight-up deterioration in the business profits due to competition, rising costs, or a shrinking customer base.

Remember, if the business is deteriorating and it isn't even managements' fault, so long as they remain in their job, they're getting paid cold, hard, cash. And they will hold onto their jobs for as long as possible by making every effort at hiding the fact they are failing or unable to bring in similar or greater profits than they did last year.

They're calling it "Adjusted Earnings" in 2019 and you will come across more named, and not useful for our purposes, figures in the so-called "Pro Forma Statements".

Will the managers go on to further evolve and begin using reverse psychology in their statements to shareholders, choosing to call their made-up numbers the "Wish We Made This Many Profits Number"? Probably not. So look out for "Adjusted", "Estimated", "Expected", "Anticipated", and other ways of saying "Money The Business Had Before Our Paychecks Were Cut."

I adore good management and custodians on the Board, this somewhat severe approach where I have taken a critical tact is only to emphasize the importance of separating the stock and its underlying business from anyone commenting on the stock.

It's better to simply *not* give management's speeches nor their numbers any credit. It doesn't have to be made up figures they deceive with; all of their forecasts about the future may be omitting negative business developments obvious to anyone.. obvious to anyone, that is, except the people who listen to management.

An Example Of Management Deception By Omission Of Information

A good example of management concealing the truth comes from the 2018 Nvidia fiasco as the stock climbed to an obscenely high valuation following the Bitcoin surge past $20,000 during December, 2017.

The background information is that Nvidia was selling a lot of what was effectively a "Pick And Shovel For Mining Cryptocurrency", it was a regular gold rush for crypto mining. Well, Bitcoin's price crashed to $7,500 by the next month (January, 2018) and Graphics Cards (GPUs) sales dried up immediately because it no longer made financial sense to invest into Nvidia cryptocurrency mining tools.

Despite the clear decline in sales, Nvidia stock continued soaring from $100 in January of 2017, to $186 during the 2017 Bitcoin peak, and the journey for Nvidia shareholders continued as the stock moved all the way up to $281 during October, 2018.

Reality was, the graphic cards sales dried up by January 1 of 2018 with the Crypto crash. This was a broken growth story for the entire duration of 2018 but didn't crash from the 3rd Quarter 2018 highs topping out at $281 per share until January of 2019, when Nvidia was trading for under $150 per share.

The Price Of A Stock You Own Will Do Whatever It Wants

Its possible for a stock you thought couldn't go any lower to, in fact, go lower. During the 1980's, Warren said to pick your stock, buy it, and be prepared for the stock to drop another 50% before recovering. This up-and-down price action is just how it is.

Prices move around more than you expect – this point speaks to both tips: *Don't sell growth stocks too soon,* and, *Don't use margin loans.* Market forces will unconsciously coordinate in order to bring the stock down, if it is to your disadvantage.

No Margin Loans

Don't use margin loans. The information that you are vulnerable to a margin call is not private and vulture funds will bring a stock down to get your margin loan called and force your firesale at 90% losses while the vulture funds will be in the market buying the stock from you at a huge discount. Maybe I am paranoid and brokers are actually mixing orders and protecting your and I's trading privacy. But who cares? The point is, don't use any margin loans because stock prices could go anywhere – I just paraphrased Warren Buffett's dictum, now I am paraphrasing again, "Be prepared for your investment's value to decline by half before it goes up to where you expect it to."

If you don't believe me about the risk of using a margin loan, just give this book to a young person you care about and start buying shares of your favorite stock on margin. Since you gave the book away and kept it off your list of assets, the brokerage won't be able to take it from you when you eventually get liquidated in a margin call and find yourself in, or nearly in, bankruptcy court. Once any probable bankruptcy proceedings have concluded, go ahead and retrieve the book from your young friend and trade it away for a crust of bread, since after the margin loan fiasco you won't have any money to invest, anyway.

Don't experience a margin loan fiasco for yourself.

The Arts And Technique Of Stock Picking

The Art Of Stock Picking For Common And Uncommon People

You want to pick stocks that are trading for a lower price today than they appear to be "valuable-at" in some future time. This is a stock picking book so sorry for the lack of personality and humanity when I am writing a technical manual to keep the reader's head screwing tighter about stocks.

The fact is, there are plenty of companies trading for $10 a pop per share and they're bringing in something like $1 per share of earnings per year. These companies are perfect candidates even though many people will write them off as normal stocks. Among these companies are a certain number who will be winning tomorrow and making just as much or more money, and there are a majority who will be shrinking or out of business. That's where the risk is.

Fantastic stock picking is the way to guard yourself from picking over priced business investments.

Remember you have an advantage as all of the stocks trading for $10 will be in a Mutual Fund, Exchange Traded Fund, Index Fund, or other Dumb Money "Whirlpool" Investment Process like the newer "automatic traders" programs from the big brokers. The advantage is the pooled money is being distributed into the stock auctions through an intermediary Wall Street Brokerage Firm, so the real auction process is being bypassed by billions of purchases going into the stocks. This is a material fact.

And the individual investor's advantage is likely to persist as there are only a few people with the smarts and information to pick stocks on their own. An up to date stock picker will probably be able to produce good stock picks clear through the year 2098.

Let's play around and use a "Deep State" fantasy to paint a picture of the risks poor people face. The government is controlled by the large money players who will push for more inflationary legislation and drive asset prices up in general. Everyone in the investment pools will make a small return while the purchase power that should be driving stock prices up will be partially diverted into the shrinking businesses by the spillover from bad robo-picks.

Meanwhile, the Wall Streeters purchase the dividend stocks while they can still provide a return on equity. The end game here is a perpetual inflation and poverty enforcement police. So its better that you start getting rich now, then you can assign your own son as head of the poverty enforcers, rather than find your son has been shot by a poverty enforcement agent while he was mowing the neighbors lawn for a $20 bill (illegal earnings mandate? Who knows what a socialist future may hold?). Enough with the fantasy. The point is, robo-advisors are not going to be able to pick stocks as well as you are once you have read this book.

And that's good news.

The shares priced at $10 for businesses earning $1 per share today is a fertile field. Many stocks are trading somewhere around this price-per-earnings ranging around $10 for $1 of annual earnings per share. The basic way to quote earnings per share is by last year's number or the running total of earnings for the trailing twelve month's time. Take the same stock picking mindset when you are looking at large and small companies. On the other hand, you have to adjust to the situation. I talk about companies trading at a price of $10 to $1 and many of the mega-sized companies have solidly traded for more than $18 per $1 earnings for years running. Adjust to the stock picking situation, not the hype.

Our preferred metric for measuring whether a business is actually making money or not is the following question's answer: Is the company bringing in more dollars than it is obligated to relinquish to the Bankers and Laborer? That's the only material criterion for our purposes. In the financial statements this intelligence is found in the Statement of Cash Flows. You want to become a master of interpreting these financial statements, or at least use the technique I outline in the next passages of this book.

Luckily there is not an arcane science lying in those financial statements, there is just book keeping and some fancy proclamations from the King Accountants that tend not to change for long periods of time, on account of the fact Accountants are lazy but partly on account of the fact the book keeping business is very old (over 2,000 years ago the Romans were keeping Merchant's Books with numbers just like we are today).

There's no reason to change what is old and working, not too often at least. You can tell its working because the rich keep getting richer, which is the natural course of things. So aim to count yourself among the rich someday.

Returning to the art of stock picking, we know artists have skills built up over long periods of time. Those skills are then combined into works of art by the artist.

Think of the prodigious drawing, painting, and engineering skills of Leonardo da Vinci. Stock picking is operating in the field of business and the good news is the following. Business is big, its everywhere, business appears to me to be doing everything outside of.. what, Church and whatever the Government has monopolized with inordinately burdensome regulations (the sticky red tape). So while it may be true the world of business is shrinking and our planet is on the way to serfdom with a few rich plutocrats. That's your dad's fault, not yours.

What you have to do now is get rich because it isn't that the world of business is becoming less our world, or more the government's possession, its that the money system is being manipulated in such a way as to risk destroying the potential for new individuals to create businesses.

Think about that. Your children are New Individuals and they may not be able to start a business, they will have to sign up for slavery (slavery is self-imposed in the developed world, and it means when you are working with no way to get rich by leveraging your earnings by taking risks, starting a new business, learning and investing, and that sort of thing). If you want to spare your children slavery, start on the path to riches today instead of just counting on it happening in the future. Otherwise, who will teach them how to attain riches? Can some book do it? Will they even learn to read intelligently?

Anticipating the direction of the world is easy. There are radio commentators saying the same things I am saying, people writing articles, and so forth. CNN wants to hide this information because the reality is unpleasant to mommies. Only mommies watch CNN, notice the trends are perfectly correlated: Fewer mommies in the U.S. coincides with CNN's 80% decline in viewership numbers since the 2000's. If CNN loses its audience they all lose their jobs, so expect fertility propaganda to arrive on CNN soon.

Consider this, my power to write these words is protected by the Constitution of these United States. Property and gun rights are also protected, but guess what, the States and Feds are still seizing property and sometimes aggrandizing the injustice by distributing the pillaged loot into administrator's budgets. Similarly, your right to privacy is being annihilated by Data Keeping Laws. Every data keeping law is in effect designed to help someone spy on your past and nit pick your activities, and are illegal in the light of a simple reading of the Constitution of our Government.

But, we let things get out of control – well, our Dad's did. All we can do now is fight on the battlefield of Moneyball until the Technology is available to replace the current Human Administered Government with Something Less Bad. This book is meant to improve the surfing conditions for you and I from here and now, clear to the somewhat more technological future.

Contemplate the following information: Between the year 2008 and the year 2010, the U.S. Dollars in the system was multiplied by Four Times. That is every dollar in your bank account was multiplied by four and you became four times richer.

Oh wait, just kidding. How that worked was that all of the Dollars in the World were tallied up, and then that total number of dollars was multiplied by Four and That Much Money was given to the biggest Corporate Banks. It all worked out fine because now you are getting .01% interest on your money and those suckers in Europe are getting -1% interest on their money. Pathetic.

So let's talk stock picking. Here are a few tricks you need to have combined with your own personal skills that you have already built up throughout your life. Maybe you have never had a job but you are good at videogames, or playing darts. That's going to be enough to combine with these Stock Picking Tricks Of The Art. Here's my bullet point list of hot tips for stock picking:

0. • Money In – Money Out = Business Earnings

1. • Make sure the company is accumulating money, not spending more than they have coming in
2. • Look for the figure Cash From Operations (first Sub Total listed on the Statement of Cash Flows), make sure that number is Plus Money and on track for More Plus Money – that means don't buy a company that had Plus money from Operations last year but its out of business this year. If they are out of business, they are not on track for more Plus Money (except for asset sales and workout scenarios – leave that for another section)

3. • Look for the Money Accumulation Thread of Reality. That is, a combination of Plus Money From Operations and less Minus Money From Investment. Cash from Investing Activities is the second sub total you will find on the Statement of Cash Flows. This will usually be a negative number mostly because of the line item called "Capital Expenditures". Take the Plus Money from Operations and subtract the Spend Money On Investment then you have an idea of whether the company made any money for the period of time covered by the Statement of Cash Flows.

   That period of covered time is marked at the top of the page and will say something like "For The Three Month Period Ended XX/XX/XXXX" or the Year period, or "For the Nine Months ended"
4. • Move down to the next Sub Total called Cash From Financing activities. The cash from financing should be 0 over long periods of time. But it will always be something besides Zero. What to do? Look at the Balance Sheet Financial Statement and approximate the company's Debt Interest Expenses by taking the Total Long Term Debt and multiply it by the Trick Interest Rate of 10% to get the Trick Interest Expense. Now, take the Trick Interest Expense and subtract that from One Year Period of Cash From Financing to get the Reified And Tricked Up Cash From Financing Figure.
5. • Now, take your subtotals from top to bottom and find out if the company is Accumulating Money or if they are a cash burning machine.

That is the formula: Money In – Money Out = Business Earnings

Cash From Operations – Cash From Investing – Tricked Up Cash From Financing = Business Earnings

..for stock picking purposes. As you become more skilled, you will learn how to Trick Up every number, but its only useful to trick up here and there.

Part of the expansion of human skill is in the inflation into new knowledge followed by the pruning of what turned out to be useless. Getting new knowledge is like breathing. If your aim is to be a master stock picker instead of a successful part time stock picker, **one way to continue the journey** is by expanding your ability to understand Tricked Numbers by working out some basic book keeping knowledge to learn why we stock pickers are forced to Trick Up the Cash From Financing numbers.

Spoiler: since we don't know what interest rates will be in the future, we want to find businesses where even a surprise increase in interest rates will not destroy the profitability of the operations.

Now you have the skill to get an idea of how a company is doing: Knowing the answer to the first question of whether the business is Profitable or Not Profitable. Are they making money or not? Stock pickers can get by just fine focusing on companies that are Profitable, according to the hot tips given above.

Now, we know the business is making $1 per share or $50 per share or $10,000 per share (like Berkshire Hathaway is). We just divide Business Earnings by the Total Number Of Shares Outstanding.

So how do we buy the stock for a low price? I used the example of the plethora of companies earning $1 per share and trading in the market for $10 per share as this is a big field to get stock picking about among the various opportunities and losers.

We know how to filter the unpickables by the Money In – Money Out = Business earnings formula, so we ditch the unpickables and look at the Various Opportunities. This, then, calls for another bullet point list of hot tips for Stock Picking from Various Opportunities..

Hot Tips for Stock Picking From Various Opportunities

• The low-or-high-price rating is the most important thing that will help you sort out the Various Opportunities. Its typically called valuation by cool people who know about stocks.

• Low prices are when the company is trading for fewer than 10 times the annual earnings you expect them to have.

• The art of stock picking is the act of evaluating whether a company is probably going to be able to keep earning the same amount of money or more money than it reported earning during the last year or ten years.

- When a company's stock price is priced below $10 for every $1 of stock picker's earnings, like I described by the Money In – Money Out = Business Earnings formula, that means the market expects that company to earn less money in the future. That's the stock picker's opportunity. A survivor company trading for less than $10 per $1 of surviving profits IS the "buy low" opportunity.
- Don't assume the market is wrong just because a company is trading at $6 for $1 of earnings. Remember, if the business is over and they shut down, there is no next year of earnings.
- The Buy Low opportunity is not when all of your friends who have not read this book are telling you about a stock going up. That is, don't lose your cool about stock picking just because of the hype.

Digressions Into The Author's Point Of View

Or, "Don't be like me, just take the information"

(Remember this is just a silly, green jacketed book)

I Figure I Will Tell You About Myself To Potentially Help You Gain Perspective

My name is Terren Richard Faloh. So, there's that.

Non-Symmetries In Life

The fact is, I don't care if you read this so long as you paid the price for the book. Money Matters. However, since you are reading this, I like you. I am glad we are getting along.

I want to point something out I believe will be useful for you. This comes from my own experience. The header says "Non-Symmetries In Life". Symmetry is easily described by geometrical methods. The Greek alphabet has a capital letter called Phi drawn like this: Φ. See how that is a circle with a line drawn through the middle of it? The left and the right of the circle are symmetrical halves of the whole circle.

To be more verbose I will list a few more reasonable views about symmetry.

Symmetry may mean equivalence, equilibrium, same-same, and, a quantifiable equivalence is present in some form. Symmetry may mean the Left side is identical to the Right side, or, the symmetry referred to may be more nuanced and contemplate some congruence between the Left and the Right side, given the complete contextualization of the matter.

To simplify a bit we'll return to symmetry by congruence and use for our example the Lotus Flower, which unfurling its petals, does create a symmetrical image although not every petal is identical. The symmetry, since it isn't about being identical, is in this case about the broad pattern those six lotus petals make as the flower blossoms.

The Art Of Stock Picking For Common And Uncommon People

Another interpretation of symmetry is that it means the One is following the same rules as the Adjacent (next-to) One.

In an entirely simple minded way, symmetry may mean the one is the same as the two. For example I might write $1 \times 2 = 2$. That's true according to the rules of algebra. There is an entirely different take available on that equation according to the rules of set theory, or any other of the many tools and inventions for handling numbers.

Remember, the one is not the two and the two ones looking at one another are seeing ones, but they are seeing one another from their own point of view. This matters for purposes of doing stuff in general.

How this became apparent in my own life requires I speak to my own humanity. So, here's the one weird thing that comes around and reminds me about the non-symmetries in life.

I have Green Eyes. Like, the iris of each of my eyeballs is the color Green.

But you know what? I have had people, various people from many walks of life, comment on my eyes. Just today, infact, the cashier at the grocery store commented,

"Your eyes are so beautiful, and they match your shirt perfectly!"

I was flattered. Anyhow, I won't recount every moment of the encounter. But, here is the message: My eyes are Green. And ninety-nine out of one hundred comments on my eyes, both when I did not ask what the other person saw, and when I did ask what the other person saw, they answer, ninety-nine times out of one hundred, is they see my eyes are Blue.

Of course, my eyes are Green and today's shirt was a baby blue tee.

The moral is..

The Art Of Stock Picking For Common And Uncommon People

What you see may not be what another sees, even if it isn't something so easily confused as One Of The Three Primary Colors Being Confused For Another.

Now imagine the miasmic number mixology of the Financial Statements a Stock Picker must interpret. Now imagine a bunch of pretend stock pickers who did not read this book and gain this knowledge. Those people will argue with you about stock picks. But they may not even be able to tell Green from Blue, when it comes to stock picking.

The non-symmetry is that we are not exactly seeing the same things around us, once you take into account our individual points of view.

So, like I wrote earlier in this book, the way to pick stocks is independently.

And anyway, if we keep printing enough money, every stock picker will be a winner.. so let the doubters slide into Newbie McSlick's shoes, or go along their merry way doing their own thing. A few of us will just happen to be Big Winners. And we'll just have to help the rest out.

Enough with the theatrics, some readers are saying. Well you are in luck, the book comes to its end here.

FIN

APPENDIX

The Art Of Stock Picking For Common And Uncommon People

The following is a Point-Reply-Point-Reply sequence with Peter Lynch, I took his points from the great investment classic One Up On Wall Street by Peter Lynch, 1988.

Understand the nature of the companies you own and the specific reasons for holding the stock ("It is really going up!" doesn't count.)

I agree.

By putting your stocks into categories you'll have a better idea of what to expect from them.

Peter Lynch uses six categories, Warren E. Buffett used three back in the day: General, Workout, and Cigar Butt. You can look the definitions of these categories for stocks up on the crazy internet thing we have in 2019 and beyond.

Big companies have small moves, small companies have big moves

This is false, a relic of a bygone age, when the ancient book was written and published during 1988. Big companies can have big, big moves, just as small companies can.

Consider the size of a company if you expect to profit from a specific product.

This is true. When you become an Advanced Number Tricker, you will understand that what matters is the Profitability the new product can Add to the bottom line. If Microsoft comes out with a Microsoft Branded Gold Bars Product they sell for a 1% profit margin, it doesn't matter how popular the product is, nor how many gold bars they sell for so small a profit margin. Point is, Microsoft earns so much from Windows and other products, that's a portfolio they have developed over a long period of time. Giant dinosaur companies such as Microsoft are an accumulation of successful products already, not a lean start up organization where the capital vehicle goes from start-up to a profit making venture. That's why its not reasonable to expect to double your money in ten years with Microsoft, then again, their being a big company doesn't mean its not a great investment at the right price.

Look for small companies that are already profitable and have proven that their concept can be replicated.

That's smart.

Be suspicious of companies with growth rates of 50 to 100 percent a year.

This is reasonable.

Avoid hot stocks in hot industries.

Yea, yea – you will find they are usually trading for $30 per $1 earnings, or $50 per $1 earnings. That's expensive.

Distrust diversifications, which usually turn out to be diworseifications.

Here, Peter Lynch is saying: Don't buy into management's speeches about growing through acquisition. More about diworseification in One Up On Wall Street.

Long shots almost never pay off.

Almost never, that's true.

The Art Of Stock Picking For Common And Uncommon People

Its better to miss the first move in a stock and wait to see if a company's plans are working out.

He is only trying to protect you from buying in at the first time a company has dropped in price, and to protect you from buying in just because the stock price has gone up for a while or vice-versa. Remember, all of this is stock price action is happening and almost nobody is using the stock picker's formula:

Money In − Money Out = Business Earnings

Stick to the principle factors of valuation and business investing. Then, prices climbing and dropping will be a sometimes entertaining, sometimes frightening side show, but you shouldn't lose any money because of the prices movements. That can only mean you were buying high and selling lower, which is not the way to do the job described in this book.

People get incredibly valuable fundamental information from their jobs that may not reach the professionals for months or even years.

This is true. Here, speaks to the core of Peter Lynch's book "One Up On Wall Street".

From my point of view, this whole book was written to tell people that there is no magic wizard of Wall Street who knows what stocks are going up or going down tomorrow or in ten years from now. If you pick stocks independently, you are actually doing better than most people on Wall Street, who have to pick stocks based on where their Banking Manager needs to get money flowing to.

Separate all stock tips from the tipper, even if the tipper is very smart, very rich, and his or her last tip went up.

This is a good warning not to tag along with people who are shouting stock picks all the time and it happens to be that one of their picks went up so that's all they want you to remember (think: CNN voodoo charter needs to make a return appearance in order to continue getting paid).

Some stock tips, especially from an expert in the field, may turn out to be quite valuable. However, people in the paper industry normally give out tips on drug stocks, and people in the health care field never run out of tips on the coming takeovers in the paper industry.

He's saying most people have not read 2019's The Art Of Stock Picking For Common And Uncommon People, which is the world where people always have a clear talk about the business earnings and $10 to $1 valuation comparison if they are talking about stock picks.

Shameless plug aside, Peter Lynch is observing how people miss out on benefiting from things they see going on around them because their attention is focused somewhere else ("people in the health care field never run out of tips [..regarding] the paper industry").

Invest in simple companies that appear dull, mundane, out of favor, and haven't caught the fancy of Wall Street.

Smart.

Moderately fast growers (20-25 percent) in nongrowth industries are ideal investments.

I agree. The stock picker needs to look at the price of the business based on the Money In – Money Out = Business Earnings formula.

Look for companies with niches.

I agree. A thing to note is this. Sometimes niches are completely dominated and all of the profit growth potential is almost gone. For example, the Soda Business is a niche dominated by Coca-Cola. They probably won't make twice as much profits in the year 2025 as they did this year, 2019, because, everyone who drinks soda or pays for water is already buying a Coca-Cola product.

Coca-Cola dominates a niche to such a great extent that the biggest risk to Coca-Cola is that a new Soda goes Viral and the business doesn't sell to Coca-Cola. So Coca-Cola's returns on stock pick potential is "a little bit up, a lotta bit down." So while I agree with Peter Lynch that a company dominating its niche is valuable, that doesn't mean they are selling for a low price like a stock picker needs to buy into it.

When purchasing depressed stocks in troubled companies, seek out the ones with the superior financial positions and avoid the ones with loads of bank debt.

This is true. Here, we are talking about turnaround situations. Its a depressed stock; sales have been declining; everyone is pessimistic; maybe the industry is showing signs they don't need the company anymore. If *that* company is also carrying a huge debt load (that means Mandatory Interest Payments), then they may not have the cash to buy the time necessary to find their path forward and large debts may cause a shaken company to go bankrupt, losing all of their investors' money and the jobs that company supports.

To reduce your risk, if you want to put some money into an entrepreneurial adventure, don't put it into one that is guaranteed to lose based on the 10% Interest Expense Trick I wrote about in Section 2: Knowledge.

The Art Of Stock Picking For Common And Uncommon People

Notes From The Author

This was the first edition of the book, and really somewhat of an early release. If you want to hear from me again, start by following my account at the online shopping website www.gumroad.com. My author page is https://gum.co/stockpicking where more updates come through relative to the Amazon page, where I will also continue publishing.

Email me at TerrenRF@tutanota.com.

Tell your friends and family about the book or whatever, to help me sell more copies of course.

Good luck and have fun.

www.ingramcontent.com/pod-product-compliance
Lightning Source LLC
Chambersburg PA
CBHW030018190526
45157CB00016B/3125